Shadowing
the Ground

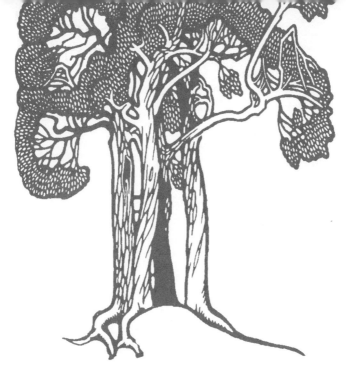

Other poetry books by David Ignatow

Poems, 1948
The Gentle Weightlifter, 1955
Say Pardon, 1962
Figures of the Human, 1964
Earth Hard: Selected Poems, 1968
Rescue the Dead, 1968
Poems: 1934–1969, 1970
Facing the Tree, 1975
Selected Poems, 1975
Tread the Dark, 1978
Whisper to the Earth, 1981
Leaving the Door Open, 1984
New and Collected Poems, 1970–1985, 1986

PROSE VOLUMES

The Notebooks of David Ignatow, 1973
Open Between Us, 1980
The One in the Many: A Poet's Memoirs, 1988

Shadowing the Ground

David Ignatow

Wesleyan University Press

Published by University Press of New England
Hanover and London

Wesleyan University Press
Published by University Press of New England, Hanover,
NH 03755
© 1991 by David Ignatow
All rights reserved
Printed in the United States of America   5   4   3   2
CIP data appear at the end of the book

Some of these poems appeared previously in *Black Warrior,
Boulevard, Caliban, Cream City Review, Exquisite Corpse, Four
Quarters, Gettysburg Review, Images, Jewish Frontier, Manhattan
Poetry Review, Marsyas, Michigan Quarterly Review, Ontario
Review, Pacific Review, Painted Bride Quarterly, Ploughshares,
Pequod, Poetry East, Practises of the Wind, Raccoon, Seneca
Review, Southern Humanities Review, West Hills Review, William
and Mary Review, Williwaw.* "I want a poem that tells itself"
appeared in *Beloit Poetry Journal,* chapbook 20, vol. 40, no. 4
(1990). "I close my eyes" and "I don't know which to mourn"
appeared in *Boulevard* (March 1991). "Now that he is aging,"
"At the water's edge of a deserted beach," and "Father fell
backwards off the stool" appeared in *Marsyas.* "We can't write
ourselves into eternal life," "If we could be brought to the
surface," and "Now I feel so far from you" appeared in *Poetry.*
"Lying between her legs" was first published in *Southern
Humanities Review,* vol. XX, no. 2 (Summer 1986).

To the memory of Paul Zweig
1935–1984

CONTENTS

ONE

Shadowing
the Ground

1

The world is so difficult to give up,
tied to it by small things,
my eyes noting movement,
color and form. I am watching,
unable to leave, for something
is happening, and so I stand
in a shower of rain
or under a hot sun, worn out
with looking.

2

Now that he is aging
there is nothing but aging.
Now that he perceives it,
there is nothing but perception;
and now that he can speak it,
aware that he has spoken,
there is nothing but awareness,
he goes about with thoughts,
awareness, and speech and is seen
to be alive.

3

More and more you are growing old.
What have you to say for yourself?
I offer my apologies to my friends
for this self-betrayal.

4

The sunlight, piercing the gloom of this house,
has pierced me to where memory lives
of a prophetic joy when I was young,
now quiescent, nearly forgotten
beneath the surface of my aging
but for the sudden entrance
of sunlight into this house.

5

Sometimes I think I've lived too long,
repeating mistakes and pleasures.
What are trees, grass, and sky to me
but emblems of the life that escapes me?
In my search for religion
I have found science;
in my search for final cause
I'm contained in its study.

6

I want a poem that tells itself
what to do: go and meet people,
convince them you desire their friendship
in a house together. Poem,
be their patient stand-in
when they kill or curse themselves.

7

This is the solution: to be happy with slaughter;
to be confident in theft; to be warm and loving
in deception; to be aesthetically pleased
with unhappiness and, in agreement,
to lie down in the blood of our innocence.

8

The other world is of the spirit
that we bring to this one
to live it through as a substance
for the spirit to dwell on
in wonder at the world
in which I take my food
and lie down to die.

The spirit is gentle
with that world it rises from
and probes, seeking for its nature
and escape to live its own life
apart but is brought back by death
as by life when life is good
and when death is better.

9

Old men spend their days farting
in private to entertain themselves
in the absence of friends
long since gone.

Old men take long walks by themselves
at a slow pace, in rhythm with their hearts,
watching themselves, death
in their trembling steps,
in mediation with their lives.

10

When I was a tiny mouselike creature, I was frightened of
    myself,
so many others were twice my size, a hoof covering me entirely
and then, as I died, leaving my bones upon the forest floor,
    I was
relieved of myself, until I discovered I had become a monkey.
    Would
I never stop becoming and be allowed to rest?

Of course, I died as a monkey in the mouth of a tiger and that,
I thought, or hoped, would be the end, killed, the life thing
    itself,
but no, I awoke to being a chimpanzee, an even larger species,
which I lamented right from the start, knowing I was doomed
to become and to become.

Well, here I am, among you men and women, and we resemble
    one another,
don't we, and we all have that sense of dissolution in us, if I
may speak for all of us. Do I have a self I can count on, if only
to escape coming apart, even as I congratulate myself,
the medium of my change? I should be proud in this beautiful
world that is changed with me. Then the world and I are one
and the same? What a delightful idea, to do with as I wish.

11

For Dan Rather

Here I am, with mike in hand, shooting down the rapids in my business suit, broadcasting to the world my sensations as I near my death. Occasionally you hear me blubber, a wave having knocked against my mouth. But it all gets said, though when I plunge over the falls the force of it will knock the mike out of my hand. In the meantime, I keep my head, reporting myself in fear, fright and elation at the experience I could have only by shortening my life. I'm enjoying it all.

12

I killed a fly
and laid my weapon next to it
as one lays the weapon of a dead hero
beside his body—the fly
that tried to mount the window
to its top; that was born out of a swamp
to die in a bold effort beyond itself,
and I am the one who brought it to an end.
Tired of the day and with night coming on
I lay my body down beside the fly.

13

Why was I born if I have to die,
buzzed the fly, and buzzed and buzzed,
and when it grew tired it rested.

14

I am leaving earth with little knowledge of it,
without having visited its great cities and lands.
I was here for a moment, it seems, to praise,
and now that I am leaving I am astounded
to have been born at all.

So what does cruelty mean in these circumstances,
and what does triumph, empire and domination,
but waves upon the still sea beneath
And what does failure mean but to sink below
into the permanence of ocean of our being.

15

Bearing leaves again,
the tree that was the skeleton of itself:
how is it I grow more tired
with each succeeding year
of bringing a poem to life?

I am not content as an old man
growing nearer to myself,
alive on earth,
a leaf in season.

16

Because words have no effect upon the wind
or the trees, I am a curious onlooker,
but I know that if I were a tree
I too would bend in the wind
and try not to despair. If I were a tree
I would want to believe the wind
had a purpose, because to save myself
would imply to stay rooted
is to stay alive.

17

The leaves of the tree hide the sun
but often enough it shows itself.
Whether it is so intended,
I myself am here by accident.

There is no mercy in things.
There is no warmth in becoming.
Trees, mountains, earth and water
will vanish in me.

18

I want to write a poem that will make me happy
enjoying the sight of broken pavement,
potholes in the street, dirty rainwater
in puddles, and traffic speeding by, splashing
clothes of passersby.

Alongside the street a cemetery older than I am,
older than twice me. Enjoy that,
enter that into my catalogue of the world.

I have acted on impulse, free to drift.
Farther on in my walk I see a railroad,
farther yet a junkyard of wrecked cars,
a cemetery of broken steel. So this is
what is meant by happiness,
to roam the streets
and come across two cemeteries,
one for humans,
one for human artifacts.

19

At the water's edge of a deserted beach,
standing between the two choices,
I contemplate my position
with an objectivity
as though the mind
lives on forever.

20

I'm going back to something
that doesn't exist, and I'm going
as if it does,
asking to be secure in death,
in the emptiness afraid to live.

21

The face of branches
lit up from behind
by a declining sun
is the sad one
of Agamemnon's daughter
who has led her brother
to his mother's death
and is not yet done
with living.

22

I close my eyes like a good little boy at night in bed, as I
was told to do by my mother when she lived, and before bed I
brush my teeth and slip on my pajamas, as I was told, and look
forward to tomorrow.

I do all things required of me to make me a citizen of sterling
  worth.
I keep a job and come home each evening for dinner. I arrive
  at the
same time on the same train to give my family a sense of order.

I obey traffic signals. I am cordial to strangers, I answer my
mail promptly. I keep a balanced checking account. Why can't I
live forever?

23

We can't write ourselves into eternal life
and that is the sorrow and waste,
but those who would write
have found a subterfuge
to let themselves be prompted,
in heady confidence of meaning:
the wealth of self spread among readers
because they have been witness
to their birth, growth, and death,
and share the earth with earth.

24

Do you know what you are doing, you fool of a cosmos, giving
me life only for a time? Have you not made a mistake, to
say the least, since it was you who made me of your
    workmanship,
of which you should be proud to have me in your likeness,
made of your powers that you have stinted in me? Are you
not ashamed to have to hear me—yours and yours alone
—complain, child of your weakness in a moment of
    self-doubt?

Hear how I speak to you in your voice and pride. I am yours
all right, and you must do as I say because I have in me
your fatherhood that must be obeyed. Now do as I demand
and do not spare me my few more years in this form but
make me at once your immortal self and blind me forever
from this wasting life.

25

Here I am
at the toilet bowl
overlooking the cemetery
and as I gaze down
at my own foregone conclusion
calmly piss.

26

Death and life are intimates
we cannot separate. We are jealous
of their relationship and fearful
of its consequences, left to live
with ourselves in isolation
with ourselves who have no one
to turn to, no relationship
as intimate.

27

The fish that lives at the bottom
has no name. It enjoys the sea
about itself and the dark, knowing
it will never leave and that, when
it ceases to exist, it will exist,
nevertheless, in the anonymity
of the sea.

28

If we could be brought to the surface
like a gleaming fish and served for supper,
if we could eat and swallow our own life
to make a good meal, if we could go fishing
for ourselves and feed on the gleaming
swimmer below the surface of our skin—
the fish that is our slippery life
and death.

TWO

29

I hear a child singing,
her father dead,
killed in a drunken brawl
with his buddies.
In the street
as she waits for her mother
to take her for a walk
she makes up songs
in which she sings his name.

30

What I had witnessed had been lived through
and died of by a young woman in labor
in the house across the street from mine
where I sat at my window and looked out
upon the still curtains of that house,
silent after the first outburst of grief.
I sat, a young man awaiting my own experience,
I would have to leave my room.

Now white-haired,
on that same street
silent
as it had always been,
its trees shadowing the ground,
I have forgotten her name.

31

On the side panel of a truck this sign:
Martin Buchbaum—Home of Quality Meat:
confusion of the living with the dead.
To eat of the living—
this makes for brotherhood.

32

I'm very well, thanks.
At this moment a million people
are dying of cholera
in Bangladesh, but I have nothing
to fear. My daughter is playing
in the yard with her kitten.
My wife is baking bread.
I've written a poem about myself.

33

White-haired, I walk in on my parents
and they, in their twenties, dark-haired
and with fresh complexions, are stunned.
I have stepped out of my crib
in the room set apart from theirs
to show myself an old man
in their youth.

I cannot spare them;
I tell them grief is pure
in what there is to know
between birth and death.

I take their hands
and lead them in a circle,
locking eyes, hands, bodies
with the past in our future.

34

Mother, how wrinkled and old must you become
before you die? How many foolish things
out of your agony must you say? In your prime
you commanded us and without prompting
we lived with you. When we were of age
we departed. In your old age, weakened
of command, reduced to complaining, you are
not the same person, and we are not the same
for it either. We too see ourselves alone,
for with love and command gone we are directed
towards ourselves, and alone now we are lonely
with everyone.

35

You who gave me birth between your sturdy legs
are dead. You who gave me food and drink
and washed my clothes, ironed my shirts,
took me shopping for a suit and coat are dead.
Now that I am old I sing you back
to stay with me, companion that you were to me
in youth, as now I gather strength to come
to where you are and rest with you.

36

Father fell backwards off the stool
and as they picked him up,
already paralyzed,
he smiled apologetically.

Every once in a while
I remember he is alive
and it amazes me: I have been
living as if alone in the world
with no one to turn to for advice
or a lecture, and yet my father
aged and dry—what could he say
to me but to show himself
in his brittle bones
as if saying,
I've had my day.

37

You may love your father
and find your image in his face
but do not take his word as final
if it is peace you are looking for.
It was your duty to reject him.
He will come back to you
in the mirror, and you will make one
with his death.

He lay upon his couch before bedtime
in a fetal position, preparing himself
to sleep when nothing else mattered
and he was bored, empty of life.

I carry on in his style
as if one life between us
were enough.

38

I would be buried beside my parents
to be told, Yes, our darling son,
it could have been better,
but we loved you. Lie down
beside us, face up to the sky.

39

When two people intimately involved begin to drift apart,
it is a continent splitting. Each will form a self separate
from the other. An ocean will lie between, and they will
signal across vast distance neither could ever cross.

40

When I look at her eyes
I know I have seen
a woman who has died;
she looks through me
to the next world.

I am drawn through
the passage she makes
to where she knows
herself for the last
time.

If I could be spared
I would live to praise
her.

I will lie down beside her in death
because it no longer is possible
in life, but I will lie beside her
in harmony with plants and animals
and with each other's silence
and with the moon and sun,
with darkness and with light.

41

You understand the lonely life I live,
your life as lonely as my own
and yet we share a single house
and often share each other's food
but keep a door upon each other
when each or either of us
must keep alone, not just to write
and think but live the solitary life
that is our life, that knows itself
in solitude and keeps
its own silent company.

We'll meet at breakfast,
when we do, when both of us
can manage out of bed
from separate rooms
to make that meeting happen
or else to meet quite casually
at noon to swap the dailies,
the news and stories and decisions
made by others, life outside
this house, the dailies shared
to keep us both informed
beyond our lives,
so much involved with life
in each of us.

Who between us
will die first,

that clue to separation
as we practice it,
to learn to live with truth
before it lives in us
as death,
and in our practice of apartness
as if to make it worth the effort
in the solitude of being,
with no difference
but in time.

Others after we are gone
will understand and live
as we in contemplation
of our life and of our death,
the mask each wears
of the other until
the mask grows old and worn.

Each day and night is ours
and we are happy
with our solitude,
our doors closed
to be the truth
that it alone
can satisfy
to make such solitude
its meaning and its cause.

42

We are an aging couple
in a house surrounded
by silence, left
to ourselves to do with
our lives as we wish
in the security of our persons,
to act as we had wanted to
since youth—freely
and spontaneously
towards one another,
given our lives'
long wish in old age,
lying in separate beds
in separate rooms.

43

I don't know which to mourn. Both have died on me, my wife and my car. I feel strongly about my car, but I am also affected by my wife. Without my car, I can't leave the house to keep myself from being alone. My wife gave me two children, both of whom, of course, no longer live with us, as was to be expected, as we in our youth left our parents behind. With my car, I could visit my children, when they are not too busy.

Before she died, my wife urged me to find another woman. It's advice I'd like to take up but not without a car. Without a car, I cannot find myself another woman. That's the sum of it.

44

Now I feel so far from you,
like an animal leaving its kill
to slink back into the woods.
I'll be gone in an instant,
sad, the work done, the soul
in need again of bright feathers
unstained by blood,
taming the sun
with their beauty.

I saw you die in me
the necessary death
of separation. We
became ourselves,
parted from one another,
and off I go now
back to beginnings
in the mess of leaves
and silences
when the leaves darken the day
and in closed fear
I worship an idol,
the self.

45

It is death to be alone.
It becomes the metaphor
of one's unimportance.

I turn on the TV and watch
colored images appear in human shapes
that talk and gesture and behave like me.

Dance with the dancers on the screen,
my mind is a dance of resemblance
to the living.

46

Lying between her legs,
he was performing an obeisance.
It was his known self,
certainly not intended
to create a child, nor to make sex
the existence. There would be
transformations of his bones and body
in regal time, time that was this
thrusting towards the sadness
of climax within an aperture
of flesh, as she who lay beneath him
heaved towards what they sought
in common and that would bring them
to such pleasure as to obliterate,
at least for then,
the knowledge of their future death.

47

I see a man under the trees
coming down the street with halting gait,
his right arm held against his chest
in a helpless position. He is aged.
His right foot drags behind him
reminds me of all I would forget
or forgive.

48

Woman, that you know of death is a blessing;
that you love me for what I am,
of this world, and will lay a hand
upon my beating heart.

49

This longing to be healed in you
each night in bed without you
is a struggle to breathe.

50

The world opens as you receive me
in the warmth and wet of my first birth,
born to be a joy to myself and to you.
I am alive to tell it
for the truth that is its own joy
as I live in two worlds at once,
yours in which I move ecstatically
and that which is the words for it.

I am alive forever, knowing of the happiness
of those yet to be, and so I feel no fear,
vanished in you. I am my own creator
ever to be and never to deny it
in the grave.

51

When my hand refuses to hold the pen
as my strength ebbs into space,
my mind will record it all,
itself receding vaguely into the dark.

It will be my last act
unless I perceive you weeping
or with blanched face. I'll manage
glancing to assure you
I am dying into what is yet unknown
and, like a first journey,
something to look forward to with dread,
of course, but also with the curiosity
of the living.

THREE

52

The world into which I was born
I mistrust. To live
is to doubt the need to live,
to think it sensible
to have remained unborn.

53

How lonely it is to live.
What am I waiting for by living,
in the morning especially,
as I awaken to the silence
of the trees?

Do I think I can write myself
out of this to form an other
who will keep me company?
That other is nothing else
but the thought of dying
to save myself from further loneliness.

54

For Betty Kray
1916—1987

Think that you are vanishing from this room.
Already you are its ghost-to-be
among strangers having drinks and talking;
already you are a memory to yourself.

I am nourished by the sound of steady rain
as something that lets me feel
I am comforted by plenitude
on which I can depend, this plenitude
that fills me once again.

55

I carry on a debate between the living
and the dead who talk to me persuasively
of peace from their graves, as persuasively
as the living who talk of making do
and living once again in dreams.

56

When one's eyes are open, one may say
if I should die suddenly and unexpectedly
I shall be happy at the last moment
of breathing, lifted beyond self-pity
and self-deceit.

. . . .

Convinced of death,
I enjoy the sunshine.
I know there is no help.

. . . .

If, when I die, I am found alone,
my legs outstretched upon the couch,
head resting upon a pillow, you'll know
I made the world I wanted,
of solitude in peace.

57

I just know I am growing near to death,
with nothing done to remake the world
a paradise. This is my deep frustration.

Smell the grass.

58

No such luck: No one will jump
Into my grave. You keep reading this
with curiosity. We are in the world
dying together, but scanning these words
you see me die alone.

59

About death, I have no compunctions.
It belongs to me.
We speak with the same voice
and shake hands; we are so alike
no one yet has told us apart.

About death, I would have no compunctions,
if it should tire of me at some moment.
I would know we had borne each other
equally, our burdens equal
with our pleasures. Death leaving
shall deprive me of my life
but then death too shall be deprived
of being.

60

We regret the sunsets and flowers we ignored,
the mountain peaks and sensitive persons,
the hurt we gave and took for granted
in full stride. Do you think,
given back our full strength,
we could do better?

Says the bible,
"The glory is god's. It is his handiwork."
That's good enough for me,
and I praise death, his doing too.

61

I must train myself to no longer exist
but as a stone lifted and thrown
to wherever I land, a new place,
a new odor to it and new sound
and action surrounding me, all this
without the thought of loss, despair,
or hope, a preparation for loss.
Such a life would be god's, if one
existed. But it is life I can assume
is god's, and I can live it.

62

What about dying?
I describe it happening
to keep my senses
occupied with living.

The poetry of my death
is inexhaustible,
like life.

63

I have lived to find out
the sun also will die,
I will die first
and in time
I will have a companion.

64

Ignatow is dying
and so is the sun.

65

I live with my contradictions
intact, seeking transcendence
but loving bread. I shrug
at both and from behind
the summer screen I look
out upon the dark, knowing
death as one form
of transcendence, but
so is life.

ABOUT THE AUTHOR

David Ignatow has published thirteen volumes of poetry and three prose collections. Born in Brooklyn, he has lived most of his life in the New York metropolitan area, at various times working as editor of *The American Poetry Review* and the *Beloit Poetry Journal*, poetry editor of *The Nation*, and co-editor of *Chelsea*. He has taught at Columbia, the New School for Social Research, the University of Kentucky, the University of Kansas, York College of the City University of New York, New York University, and Vassar College.

The National Institute of Arts and Letters has presented to Mr. Ignatow an award "for a lifetime of creative effort." His work has been recognized also with the Bollingen Prize, two Guggenheim Fellowships, the Wallace Stevens fellowship from Yale University, the Rockefeller Foundation fellowship, the Poetry Society of America's Shelley Memorial Award, and an award from the National Endowment for the Arts. He is president emeritus of the Poetry Society of America and a member of the executive board of the Walt Whitman Birthplace Association, Huntington, Long Island. His home is in East Hampton, Long Island.

His most recent books were *New and Collected Poems* and *The One in the Many: A Poet's Memoirs*.

ABOUT THE BOOK

The typeface used in this book is Galliard, a contemporary rendering of a classic typeface prepared for Mergenthaler in 1978 by the British type designer Matthew Carter. The book was composed by Marathon Typography Service, Inc., Durham, North Carolina. The design is by Kachergis Book Design, Pittsboro, North Carolina.

The University Press of New England
is a consortium of universities in New England dedicated to
publishing scholarly and trade works by authors from member
campuses and elsewhere. The New England imprint signifies
uniform standards for publication excellence maintained without
exception by the consortium members. A joint imprint of Univer-
sity Press of New England and a sponsoring member acknowl-
edges the publishing mission of that university and its support
for the dissemination of scholarship throughout the world. Cited
by the American Council of Learned Societies as a model to be
followed, University Press of New England publishes books under
its own imprint and the imprints of Brandeis University, Brown
University, Clark University, University of Connecticut, Dartmouth
College, University of New Hampshire, University of Rhode
Island, Tufts University, University of Vermont, and Wesleyan
University.

Library of Congress Cataloging-in-Publication Data
Ignatow, David, 1914–
    Shadowing the ground / David Ignatow. — 1st ed.
        p.   cm. — (Wesleyan poetry)
    ISBN 0-8195-2195-7 (cl). — ISBN 0-8195-1197-8 (pa)
    I. Title.   II. Series.
PS3517.G53S5   1991
811'.54—dc20   90-20872